TECHNOLOGY IN
THE ANCIENT WORLD

TECHNOLOGY IN
MESOPOTAMIA

CHARLIE SAMUELS

Gareth Stevens
Publishing

Please visit our website, www.garethstevens.com. For a free color catalog of all our high-quality books, call toll-free 1-800-542-2595 or fax 1-877-542-2596.

Library of Congress Cataloging-in-Publication Data

Samuels, Charlie.
Technology in ancient Mesopotamia / by Charlie Samuels.
   p. cm. — (Technology in the ancient world)
Includes index.
ISBN 978-1-4339-9641-2 (pbk.)
ISBN 978-1-4339-9642-9 (6-pack)
ISBN 978-1-4339-9640-5 (library binding)
1. Iraq—Civilization—To 634—Juvenile literature. 2. Technology—Iraq--History—To 634—Juvenile literature. I. Samuels, Charlie, 1961-. II. Title.
T16.S25 2014
935—dc23

Published in 2014 by
Gareth Stevens Publishing
111 East 14th Street, Suite 349
New York, NY 10003

For Brown Bear Books Ltd:
Editorial Director: Lindsey Lowe
Managing Editor: Tim Cooke
Children's Publisher: Anne O'Daly
Art Director: Jeni Child
Designer: Lynne Lennon
Picture Manager: Sophie Mortimer

Picture Credits
Front Cover: Shutterstock: main; **Thinkstock:** Dorling Kindersley RF br.

akg-images: Erich Lessing 13; **Alamy:** Ancient Art & Architecture 37, Zev Radov/BibleLandPictures 32, The Art Archive 40, Adam Woolfitt/Robert Harding Picture Library 36; **British Museum:** 25; **Corbis:** Bettmann 22, Lebrecht Music & Arts 24; **Getty Images:** DEA/G. Dagli Orti 10, Steve McAlister 43; **istockphoto:** 4; **Public Domain:** Lasse Jensen 19; **Shutterstock:** 20, Aantonio Abrignani 9, 11, Kamira 30, 31, Jerry Rainey 17, Styve Reineck 12, Opis Zagreb 8; **Thinkstock:** Dorling Kindersley RF 23, 26, 35, Hemera 28, 34, istockphoto 33, Photos.com 27, 29, 38.

All other artwork © Brown Bear Books Ltd

Brown Bear Books has made every attempt to contact the copyright holder. If you have any information please contact smortimer@windmillbooks.co.uk

Manufactured in the United States of America

CPSIA compliance information: Batch #CS13GS. For further information contact Gareth Stevens, New York, New York at 1-800-542-2595.

CONTENTS

INTRODUCTION

The Mesopotamians who lived in what is now Iraq lacked many important resources. They had little wood, for example, and almost no metals. But they did have mud from the banks of the Tigris and Euphrates Rivers—lots and lots of mud. They used the mud to make bricks to build some of the world's first cities and to make clay tablets for the world's first writing. Through their cleverness and skill, the Mesopotamians built the world's first urban culture.

Because the Mesopotamians used so much mud, which dries and crumbles over time, few of their buildings remain. But their influence is everywhere. Not only did they invent the first cities and writing, they were also the

The lion became the symbol of Babylon in the seventh century B.C.E., during the city's second major period of importance.

The Gate of Ishtar was the main gate of the city of Babylon. It was dedicated to the city's main goddess.

first people to use the wheel. They invented the zodiac and one of the earliest calendars. They learned to cast bronze and iron objects, and to make glass.

SERIES OF POWERS

There was no single country called Mesopotamia. The term is used to describe the region between the Tigris and Euphrates Rivers. From around 3500 B.C.E. the importance of different city-states rose and fell. In broadly chronological order, these city-states included Ur and Uruk, Sumer, Akkad, Babylon, and Assyria. The Mesopotamian period ended soon after 331 B.C.E., when Alexander the Great conquered the region. This book will introduce you to the most important examples of the technologies invented and used by these various powers of Mesopotamia.

TECHNOLOGICAL BACKGROUND

Mesopotamia has been called the "cradle of civilization." It was where many great technological advances were made. Before the Mesopotamians, people lived as nomadic hunter-gatherers. They lived in temporary structures or caves, used basic stone tools, and wore clothes made from animal skins. The Mesopotamians changed all this. Their influence was absorbed and built upon by many later civilizations.

The Mesopotamians built the first cities. They used the seasonal flooding of the Euphrates and Tigris Rivers to create

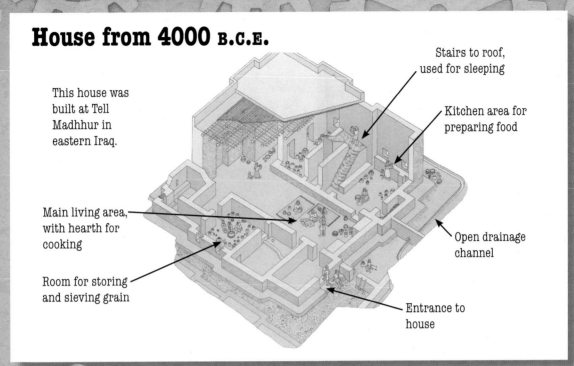

House from 4000 B.C.E.

This house was built at Tell Madhhur in eastern Iraq.

Stairs to roof, used for sleeping

Kitchen area for preparing food

Open drainage channel

Main living area, with hearth for cooking

Room for storing and sieving grain

Entrance to house

The first Mesopotamians were hunter-gatherers. They began living in round huts around 10,000 B.C.E.

a network of canals and an irrigation system to grow crops. They used the mud from the rivers to make bricks for building and clay for pottery. They figured out that the bitumen (tar) that seeped out of the earth could be used as fuel in their kilns.

PIONEER PEOPLES

In many areas, the Mesopotamians had no real predecessors. They invented technology for themselves, such as writing or using astronomy to develop a calendar. But they also interacted with other civilizations through trade, such as the Egyptians and Phoenicians. The Mesopotamians constantly exchanged ideas and learned from their neighbors, who learned from them in turn.

RIVERS AND CANALS

Mesopotamia means "the land between the rivers." The Tigris and Euphrates were the basis of Mesopotamian civilization. They watered land for farming. Mud from the river banks was used to make bricks to build cities. But it was difficult to tell when the rivers would flood.

The Euphrates River runs through a barren landscape. The river's flood is not as predictable as that of a river such as the Nile.

Merchants paddle a raft on the Euphrates in the 19th century. Rivers have been major highways in the region for millennia.

Both rivers usually flooded between April and June. Sometimes, a huge flood altered a river's course and washed away villages. In other years, the flood did not happen at all. In the north, where it did not rain often, the people saved river water by building canals to collect it.

CANAL NETWORK

Workers built thousands of canals in the desert to store water. They constructed raised earth banks near the rivers and diverted water into the channels. As the population grew, the canal network expanded. The canals regularly silted up. Workers cleared the silt with copper-bladed shovels and carried it away in baskets made from reed.

TECHNICAL SPECS

- The sources of the Euphrates and Tigris lie in the mountains of present-day Turkey.
- The banks of the Tigris are steeper than those of the Euphrates.
- The Tigris flows faster than the Euphrates, so less silt builds up in it.
- Silt raised the bed of the Euphrates so it was higher than the nearby Tigris. At Babylon, water flowed from the Euphrates to the Tigris along a canal through the city.
- The landscape of northern Mesopotamia was semiarid desert. Irrigation turned it into a region of marshes, mud flats, lagoons, and reed banks.
- Both rivers empty into the Persian Gulf.

FARMING AND IRRIGATION

In this wall carving, workers cut barley with sickles while men catch fish in a river or canal.

Farming began as early as 10,000 B.C.E. in the hilly areas near the edges of Mesopotamia, where rainfall was higher. It only became possible to grow crops on the plains at the heart of Mesopotamia when artificial irrigation was invented. Farmers controlled the flow of water through a series of dams.

Early farmers used sticks and hoes to turn the soil. The wooden plow was invented in Mesopotamia around 3500 B.C.E. The plow transformed farming. Much larger areas of land could be prepared to grow crops such as barley.

IRRIGATION

Irrigation was controlled by a series of canals and mud banks. Water was lifted to the fields using a shaduf. This was a bucket attached to a pole that worked as a lever. The shaduf was invented in Mesopotamia before 2000 B.C.E. It was later adopted by the ancient Egyptians.

TECHNICAL SPECS

- Land close to the rivers was fertile and easy to farm. Further away, it was dry and uninhabited.
- The plow was invented in China around the same time it was invented in Mesopotamia.
- Laws required all Mesopotamians to help repair canals or to build new ones.
- Some canals were over 1,000 years old.
- Farmers harvested their crops with sickles.
- Popular crops were barley, onions, apples, grapes, and turnips.
- Salt was a major problem for farmers. Too much salt on the land meant crops failed.

Shadufs are still used in West Asia to lift water for irrigation. This illustration of a group of shadufs was drawn in the 19th century.

WATER

The ancient Mesopotamians knew how important it was to have clean water. Most water came from the two major rivers, the Tigris and Euphrates, and the network of canals. Major cities were built close to a source of water. Other cities relied on springs, wells, aqueducts, or cisterns for their water supply.

The Mesopotamians invented wooden waterwheels. Similar wheels, called norias, are still used to power machines in parts of the region.

A carved stone staircase winds down into an ancient well near the site of the city of Nimrud.

In the city of Nimrud, wells were dug 90 feet (27.5 m) deep. The wells meant the city would have access to clean water if it was besieged. King Sennacherib built a stone aqueduct to carry water 6 miles (9.6 km) to Nineveh. It was fed by streams, so the city had a constant fresh water supply.

SEWAGE SYSTEM

By 2000 B.C.E., royal palaces and the homes of the wealthy had indoor toilets. These were placed against an outside wall and consisted of a seat over a hole leading to a terracotta pipe. The pipe carried sewage to a river through a system of drains that ran beneath the streets.

TECHNICAL SPECS

- The well at Nimrud could provide 5,000 gallons of water a day.
- Water was pulled up from the bottom of the well using a chain of clay pots on a pulley wheel.
- The aqueduct at Nineveh was made from stone. Water flowed over its surface, which was made from hardened earth, waterproofed by bitumen, and lined with stone.
- A typical bathroom had a floor made from baked bricks waterproofed with bitumen. A seat hid the hole of the toilet, which was flushed using a jug of water.
- Waterwheels may have existed as early as 4000 B.C.E. They were the first machines to create mechanical energy without relying on the energy of animals or humans.

POTTERY

Ancient Mesopotamia did not have many natural resources. It lacked stone, wood, and many metals. But it had lots of clay. Clay formed the basis of its civilization. This clay was not only used to make pots and containers. It also allowed writing to be invented and cities to be built.

A potter makes a vessel from a coil of clay, which he will smooth together. Other vessels were made by pressing clay into molds.

The first Mesopotamians shaped clay pots by hand and left them to harden in the sun. Around 4500 B.C.E. they invented a potter's wheel. Around 2000 B.C.E. they invented a faster wheel rotated by foot. It meant pots could be made faster and with thinner walls. From 1500 B.C.E. pots were glazed. That made them stronger and more waterproof, as well as being decorative.

MUD BRICKS

The first bricks were made from clay mixed with straw. The bricks were dried in the sun. They were used to build not just homes, but also the ziggurats that rose above the cities.

TECHNICAL SPECS

- Early pots were made from coils or slabs of clay smoothed together.
- The potter's wheel made the walls of pots more uniform in thickness with fewer air bubbles, so they were less likely to break when they were fired.
- The Mesopotamians used sticks, bones, teeth, and shells to engrave pots before they dried.
- Before glazes were invented, potters rubbed the outside of pots with smooth stones to create a matte sheen.
- Glaze was applied with brushes made from animal hair.

A man rolls a cylinder seal over a clay tablet that will be tied to a storage jar to show who owns it.

BUILDING

By around 600 B.C.E., Babylon was one of the largest cities in the world. By then, it was already over a thousand years old.

The structure of buildings in ancient Mesopotamia depended on the available building materials. In the flat desert landscape, there were few trees to provide wood and little stone, particularly in the south. But there was lots of mud that could be shaped into mud bricks. There was also ample sunshine to dry the bricks out. Mud bricks became the most common building material.

The richer a person, the bigger the house they built. The homes of the wealthy were three stories high and had many rooms. All houses had a thick outer wall of mud bricks. There were no outside windows. This helped to ensure privacy and also kept the house cool during the day.

HOME ARRANGEMENT

Inside the home, the rooms were arranged around a central courtyard. This helped to keep the house cool. Roofs were made from the trunks of palm trees, if they were available. These beams were covered with a layer of reed and palm-leaf matting that was coated with mud to seal and smooth it.

Brick

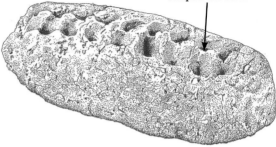

The worker's fingers have left imprints where he shaped the brick.

TECHNICAL SPECS

- Mud bricks were made by hand. Workers molded mud mixed with chopped reeds or animal dung.
- Bricks were usually dried in the sun. Some bricks were fired in hot ovens to make them water resistant. They were used for public buildings, not homes.
- In the city of Ur, builders used naturally occurring bitumen as mortar to hold bricks together.
- Liquid mud was used both as mortar and as plaster for sealing and smoothing the walls.
- If wood was available, it was used for doors.
- Clay or stone were used to create drains and door frames.

Mud is pressed into wooden molds to be dried as bricks. In the Americas, sun-dried bricks were called adobe.

CITIES

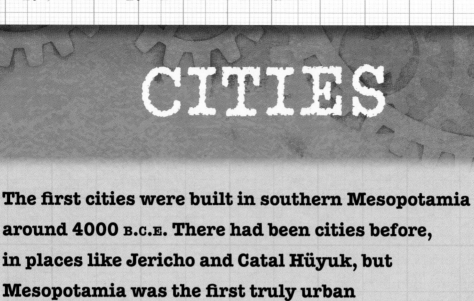

The first cities were built in southern Mesopotamia around 4000 B.C.E. There had been cities before, in places like Jericho and Catal Hüyuk, but Mesopotamia was the first truly urban civilization. By 3450 B.C.E., much of the population lived in densely packed cities surrounded by walls.

This is a market in the shadow of a ziggurat. Before coins were invented in the seventh century B.C.E., payment was usually made in grain.

People probably lived in cities because of the need for water. People had to cooperate to store water and irrigate the land, so they lived in groups. Before 3000 B.C.E., the Euphrates River changed course. Many villages were abandoned, and more people moved to the cities.

CITIES OF MUD

The first important city, Uruk, was built around 2700 B.C.E. Like other cities, it was protected by a wall of mud bricks. There were no stone buildings. Each city had its own ruler and god, to whom the city's ziggurat was dedicated.

The ruins of the ziggurat are all that remain of the ancient city of Ur. The mud-brick buildings have crumbled.

TECHNICAL SPECS

- Uruk was divided into three zones: one-third was housing, one-third was for temples, and one-third was used for gardens.
- The ziggurat at Uruk was made of mud bricks with layers of reeds and matting between the brickwork.
- Most city streets were unpaved. They were used by people to dump trash and sewage. When the street was full of debris, the people covered it with a layer of mud. As the street level rose, people built steps to reach their doorways.
- Archaeologists in Uruk have discovered what seems to have been an early drainage system.

ZIGGURATS

Rising high above the flat plain, stepped, pyramid-shaped ziggurats dominated Mesopotamian cities. The ziggurat was a physical representation of a sacred mountain. The first ziggurat was built around 2000 B.C.E. The design was copied and adapted by later civilizations, such as the Egyptians. Ziggurats became the models for Egyptian pyramids and temples.

The ziggurat of Ur has been re-created. Huge stone staircases led to the top of the ziggurat.

Ziggurats were temples. The ancient Sumerians believed powerful gods lived in the sky. They wanted to build tall structures to reach the heavens. They did not know how to build pyramids, so they built a series of platforms. Each step was smaller than the story beneath.

STONE MOUNTAIN

Ziggurats had a temple on top. Religious ceremonies were held there to honor the gods. The core of the building was made from mud bricks. To make the outside weatherproof, burned bricks were used, held together with bitumen mortar.

Workers make and carry mud bricks, while others carry reeds to be laid between the layers of a ziggurat.

TECHNICAL SPECS

- The first ziggurat was built by Ur-Nammu, who ruled Ur from 2112–2095 B.C.E.
- Bitumen mortar was one of the great inventions of the Mesopotamians. It was made from bitumen—petroleum—that seeped out of the ground. This was the first use of oil in the Middle East.
- Ziggurats could be built with or without staircases.
- Ziggurats were built from a solid core of unfired mud bricks and an outer layer of fired bricks. These were often glazed and colored.
- Terraces were filled with plants and trees in containers.
- Drains carried the water away from the upper levels.

HANGING GARDENS OF BABYLON

This is an artist's impression of how the Hanging Gardens might have appeared. No one knows what they really looked like.

The famed Hanging Gardens of Babylon disappeared 2,000 years ago. That has not stopped people from trying to imagine what they looked like. It is said that King Nebuchadnezzar II built an artificial "mountain" of mud bricks covered with large trees and bushes.

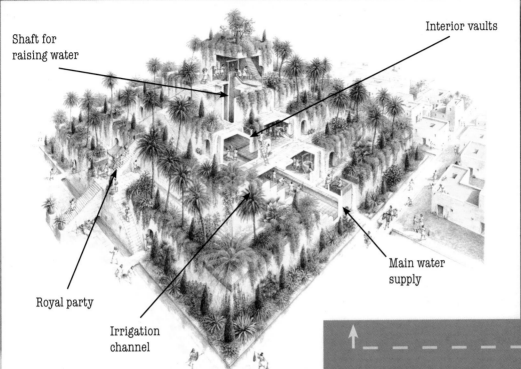

Shaft for raising water

Interior vaults

Royal party

Main water supply

Irrigation channel

Hanging Gardens

The builders faced two technical problems. How were the plants watered? And how were the clay bricks kept dry?

SOLVING PROBLEMS

Archaeologists believe water was taken from the Euphrates River. A chain pump carried water to a pool at the top of the gardens. Gates opened to send the water into channels that watered the gardens. To stop the clay bricks from getting damp, the plants grew in containers lined with stone, reeds, bitumen, tiles, and lead. No water could seep out.

TECHNICAL SPECS

- The terraces were supported on arched vaults, or hollow spaces, held up by columns.
- Unusual for Mesopotamia, the gardens were said to be built using stone slabs.
- A chain pump was a series of buckets on a chain looped around two wheels. The bottom wheel sat in a pool of water. As it turned, the buckets dipped into the water and carried it to the upper wheel, where they tipped the water out.
- Some accounts describe how water was raised up the mountain by a mechanical device called an Archimedes screw, a spiral rotating inside a sloping tube.

TRANSPORTATION

The Marsh Arabs of what is now Iraq still use boats made out of waterproofed reeds. They also use reeds to build their homes.

The best way to move around in Mesopotamia was by water. Boats sailed on the Tigris and Euphrates and on the canals. Cargo ships sailed in the Red Sea, Indian Ocean, and Persian Gulf. Roads were unpaved, so wheeled transport was not always practical. Sleds were more useful for moving heavy loads.

BOAT BUILDING

Different boats were used for different purposes. For sea journeys, the Sumerians built boats out of wood. The Akkadians built two kinds of boats. The *quppu* was like a circular basket covered with animal hides. It was paddled on the Tigris River.

The Akkadians also used a raft called a *kalakku*. It was made from bundles of reeds on top of inflated goatskins. It floated downriver with the current. When the boat reached its destination, the kalakku was dismantled. The skins were deflated and loaded on a donkey to travel back north to be reused.

TECHNICAL SPECS

- To cross rivers and canals, people used floats made from reeds and inflated goatskins.
- To inflate a goatskin, the neck and three legs were tied tightly together. The swimmer blew into the fourth leg to keep it afloat.
- In the 18th century B.C.E., soldiers in the Assyrian army were issued with goatskins for this purpose.
- On land, porters, donkeys, and mules transported goods. Local trips were made in wheeled carts.
- Boats from the Royal Cemetery at Ur (about 2600 B.C.E.) are the same shape as the reed boats used by the Marsh Arabs of southern Iraq today. The boats are waterproofed with bitumen.

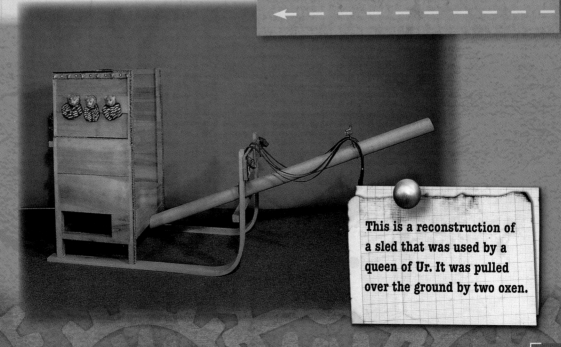

This is a reconstruction of a sled that was used by a queen of Ur. It was pulled over the ground by two oxen.

THE WHEEL

Early wheel

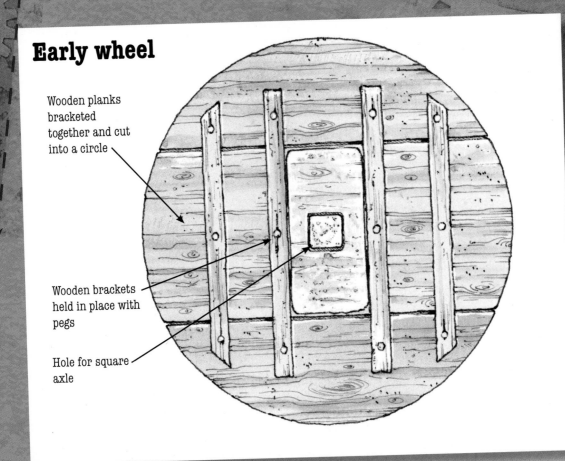

Wooden planks bracketed together and cut into a circle

Wooden brackets held in place with pegs

Hole for square axle

The wheel was invented more than once in history. The first wheels were probably potter's wheels. The earliest wheel used for transportation was invented in ancient Mesopotamia around 3200 B.C.E. Many archaeologists see the use of a wheel that rotated on a fixed axle as being one of the defining features of a civilization.

As early as 3200 B.C.E., the Sumerians of Mesopotamia made pictures of carts with solid wheels. The wheels were made from two pieces of wooden plank, bracketed together and cut into a circular shape. Wooden axles passed through the center of the circle and were held in place by lynchpins. The Sumerians used this kind of wheel for war chariots.

ADAPTABLE ARENA

By 2000 B.C.E., the Sumerians had invented spoked wheels. Spokes joined the axle to an outer wheel rim. This made chariots much lighter and easier to maneuver.

TECHNICAL SPECS

- In addition to transportation, wheel technology was also used in the potter's wheel and, from the first century B.C.E., in the waterwheel.
- The transportation wheel may have been based on the logs used to roll sledges carrying loads. As the object moved forward, the log rollers were taken from behind and replaced in front.
- The tall trees needed to make rollers and wheels were not common in ancient Mesopotamia. No one knows where the wood came from.
- The ancient Egyptians took Mesopotamian wheel technology and improved upon it.

Early potter's wheels were turned by hand. The wheel spun slowly, so the walls of pots were quite thick.

ASTRONOMY AND ASTROLOGY

The ancient Mesopotamians believed that they could tell the future by watching the skies. From the second millennium B.C.E., priests studied the night sky and noted the position of the planets and stars and the phases of the moon. From their observations of the skies, the Mesopotamians worked out a calendar. They also devised the first zodiac, which was based on groups of stars called constellations.

The Mesopotamians invented the zodiac based on the constellations. They used the zodiac to try to predict the future.

Mesopotamians believed there was a direct link between the heavens and what happened on Earth.

From studying the moon, Sumerian astronomers worked out a lunar calendar. Later, the Babylonians could predict events such as eclipses, which they thought were bad omens. Assyrian astronomers compiled a list of the positions of the stars.

THE ZODIAC

Careful observation of the skies led to the invention of the zodiac. This marked a change from compiling predictions for the king or state to predicting the future of the individual. By the fifth century B.C.E., the circular zodiac belt had been created, with 12 signs. Each sign occupied 30 degrees of the 360 degrees of the circle.

TECHNICAL SPECS

- Astronomical tablets found in Nineveh date from 700 B.C.E.
- The Sumerian calendar had 12 months of 30 days. To balance the 360-day lunar calendar with the 365.25-day solar year, they added extra days every three years.
- A Sumerian cuneiform tablet from 4000 B.C.E. describes the sighting of an exploding star.
- The first known baby horoscope was cast for a child born on April 29, 410 B.C.E.
- Assyrian astronomers used tubes as viewfinders and measured time with water clocks and sundials.
- An eclipse obscured by clouds was not seen as a bad omen.

WRITING

Of all the inventions of the ancient world, perhaps the most important was that of writing, which first appeared in Sumer. The origins of writing lay with the Sumerians' desire to keep records of their cattle, sheep, and crops. They did this from 3300 B.C.E. by drawing simple pictures on soft clay tablets. A bull's head stood for cattle, and an ear of barley stood for grain.

Cuneiform means wedge-shaped. It refers to the shape of the marks made by the stylus in the clay.

The Mesopotamians had plenty of clay for tablets, and they made wedge-shaped "pens" from reeds.

TECHNICAL SPECS

- The earliest known examples of writing date from 3300 B.C.E. They were found on clay tablets from Uruk.
- The early writing system had more than 700 different signs.
- Clay tablets were put inside a clay "envelope," so they could not be tampered with.
- Cuneiform could be read from left to right or top to bottom, depending on how it was written.
- Merchants used cylinder seals to imprint a design on soft clay to show that goods or transactions were genuine.

The early pictures changed into curved lines and then into cuneiform. These wedge-shaped characters were easy to press into clay. Around 3100 B.C.E., people began using signs to stand for sounds as well as objects. This was the real start of writing.

THE ALPHABET

Between 1700 and 1500 B.C.E., the first alphabet appeared in ancient Palestine and Syria. The Mesopotamians created a cuneiform alphabet around 1000 B.C.E. There were more than 600 cuneiform signs. Originally used for record keeping, writing was soon also used for stories, laws, spells, and recipes.

NUMBERS, WEIGHTS, AND MEASURES

The Mesopotamians invented two number systems for keeping count. The decimal system uses the number 10. It is the system we still use today. It was initially probably based on counting using the 10 fingers. The sexagesimal system uses base 60. It is the reason we still have 60 minutes in an hour. The Mesopotamians also had standard units of weight, length, and volume.

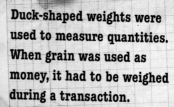

Duck-shaped weights were used to measure quantities. When grain was used as money, it had to be weighed during a transaction.

The Mesopotamians used a simple balance. Whatever was being weighed was put on one side, and a weight was put on the other.

Numbers greater than 10 were first used in Mesopotamia around 3000 B.C.E. (numerals were first used in Egypt around 3400 B.C.E.). The Mesopotamians pressed numbers into wet clay with reed pens. They used Pythagoras's theorem to work out the area of triangles 1,000 years before Pythagoras lived. They used base 60 to calculate a 360-degree circle, as well as minutes and seconds.

STANDARD WEIGHTS

Weights were standardized in the city of Ur around 2000 B.C.E. Granite weights, in the shape of a duck, were used by merchants and buyers to ensure that the goods they were buying and selling were of a standard size.

TECHNICAL SPECS

- Surviving clay tablets contain students' exercises in calculation, plus multiplication tables.
- The Mesopotamians did not use zero.
- An hour was divided into 60 minutes and a minute into 60 seconds.
- The day was divided into 12 hours of daylight and 12 hours of night (each was one-fifth of 60).
- The Babylonian mile was the equivalent of 7 miles (11 km).

WEAPONS AND WARFARE

Assyrian archers and spear carriers defend a city from the top of its walls. Sieges were a common form of warfare between states.

Warfare was a feature of Mesopotamian life. The first recorded war was around 2500 B.C.E., between the cities of Lagash and Umma. City-states fought over farmland and water. They built walls to protect their cities. The Sumerians had the first professional army.

Early weapons were based on hunting weapons and were made from wood and stone. By 4000 B.C.E., copper was being used to make axes, spears, and daggers. Bronze weapons appeared around 3000 B.C.E. and iron weapons around 1000 B.C.E.

SIEGES

Cities defended themselves with city walls. To defeat enemy cities, armies used siege weapons, such as battering rams and siege towers, from about 1000 B.C.E. Around 1500 B.C.E., the first two-wheeled, horse-drawn war-chariots were used. They revolutionized warfare.

TECHNICAL SPECS

- Horses were used 4,000 years ago to carry military equipment.
- Soldiers wore armor made from tiny overlapping pieces of bronze, like scales, sewn on to a tunic.
- The Assyrians introduced cavalry units. They rode bareback, as the saddle had not yet been invented.
- The Assyrian army had up to 50,000 troops, most of whom were infantry or foot soldiers.
- Chariots were manned by a charioteer and an archer.
- Sargon the Great of Akkad (2335–2279 B.C.E.) was the first ruler to properly train and equip an army of professional soldiers.

This relief shows a chariot being pulled by two horses as an archer takes aim. The chariot allowed archers to get far closer to the enemy.

CRAFTS

The Mesopotamians were skilled at crafts. They made objects not just out of clay but also out of stone, glass, metal, and precious and semiprecious stones. Stone and metal were often imported, but the Mesopotamians had a ready supply of fuel to heat their kilns to bake raw materials into lasting objects.

These long-necked glass vessels were made in Ur in the Sumerian period, around 1400 B.C.E.

Cuneiform records say that glass was made during Sumerian times. In fact, no glass has been found from earlier than 1500 B.C.E. But as early as the fourth and third millennia B.C.E., Mesopotamians experimented with chemicals such as lime soda and silicates. Mixing those with minerals led to the discovery of brightly colored glass. Craftspeople used glass to make containers, beads, small figures, and parts of statues.

STONE CARVING

The Mesopotamians were skilled carvers. They carved statues of their gods and goddesses out of marble and limestone. The Assyrians carved stone reliefs for their palaces. These stone pictures usually showed figures in profile and depicted rituals and mythological scenes.

TECHNICAL SPECS

- Glass was worked into shape before it cooled and hardened. It was rolled into sheets, turned into tubes, or pressed into molds.
- In reliefs, figures were carved according to importance. The king was always bigger than his courtiers, who were bigger than everyone else.
  - Statues and reliefs were finished with semiprecious stones, such as lapis lazuli for blue eyes.
  - Jewelers beat leaf metal into thin strips and added stones such as agate and jasper. Such imported stones were highly valued.

This ribbed glass vessel comes from Ur. It was glazed with colored geometric decorations.

METALS AND MINING

Mesopotamia had few deposits of metals, but metals were still very important. The ancient Mesopotamians imported ores from which to extract metals. This led to long-distance trade with other ancient civilizations, such as the peoples of the Indus Valley.

Copper did occur naturally in Mesopotamia. As early as the fourth millennium B.C.E, craftsmen smelted copper to make objects. The copper may have come from the Timna Valley in the south.

This helmet was made from electrum, an alloy of silver and gold. The metalworker then dissolved the silver, so the surface looked like gold.

HOW TO...

In the "lost wax" process, a model was made out of wax, then packed in clay to make a mold. The mold was heated so the wax melted and drained through holes. Molten metal was poured into the mold, filling the space left by the "lost wax." It was left to cool and harden. The clay was broken open to reveal the new object.

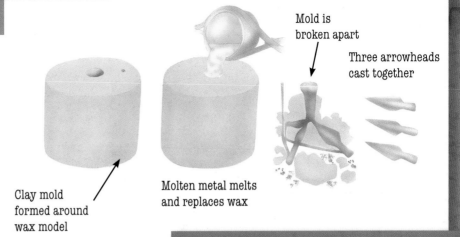

Mold is broken apart

Three arrowheads cast together

Clay mold formed around wax model

Molten metal melts and replaces wax

Most objects were a mixture, or alloy, of copper and arsenic. The alloy was easier to cast and harder than pure copper. Copper was popular up to sometime before 3000 B.C.E., when the Sumerians learned how to make bronze.

BRONZE AGE

The Sumerians made bronze by adding tin to copper. Bronze had a lower melting point, so it was easier to cast in different shapes. It was also harder and longer lasting, so it made better tools and weapons. The Mesopotamians also made objects from imported ore, including gold, silver, and lead. They invented the "lost wax" process for casting more complex shapes, such as statues, arrowheads, tools, and other weapons.

TECHNICAL SPECS

- Blades for knives were made by carving a shape into the face of a flat stone. Copper was heated and poured into the stone mold, where it cooled and was then removed.
- Furnaces were similar to the kilns used to fire pottery.
- Workers used bellows made from animal skin to pump air into furnaces. This made the fire burn hotter, so that copper could be melted and poured as molten metal.
- Fuel for the furnaces was provided by the bitumen that seeped out of the ground.
- The Mesopotamians used silver to make an early form of money. These tokens, called "shekels," were not coins, but ingots of a standard weight.

WEAVING AND DYEING

This carving shows a woman using a simple loom to weave cloth. The vertical loom was invented in the third millennium B.C.E.

Over time, people in ancient Mesopotamia went from wearing the skins from sheep and goats to wearing handwoven garments that were finished with embroidery and appliqué. The technique of spinning yarn and weaving it into textiles was known long before 3000 B.C.E. The main fabrics used were wool and linen.

A scribe counts goods as a donkey caravan arrives in Mesopotamia carrying textiles and tin from Iran.

In Sumer, people plucked sheep for wool; later they started shearing them. Men often wore belted sheepskins that came to their ankles; women wore a toga-like garment.

SPINNING

Spinning and weaving flax to make linen was done by women on flat looms. Later upright looms had ceramic weights to keep the yarn tense. They were used to weave linen. Textiles were often dyed using animal, plant, or mineral extracts.

TECHNICAL SPECS

- Linen was used only for high-quality garments worn by priests or to be placed on statues of gods.
- Felt was made from pressed low-quality wool or goat hair. It was used for shoes.
- By the third millennium B.C.E., the Mesopotomians had invented the vertical loom.
- In the eighth century B.C.E. rulers in Nimrud were buried with cloth decorated with appliqué, or pieces of another cloth sewn on.
- No word for tailor existed before the neo-Babylonian period. This may mean that making clothes was only seen as a special skill late in Mesopotamian history.

MEDICINE

Medical practitioners existed as early as the third millennium B.C.E. Cuneiform tablets from the library of Ashurbanipal, the last Assyrian king of Nineveh, reveal what the Mesopotamians knew about sickness and how they treated the sick. They describe two kinds of doctors: the asipu and the asu.

Priests use spells to try to cure a patient. They are dressed as fish so they can appeal to the god of water.

This tablet lists illnesses and remedies, which made use of plant, mineral, and animal extracts.

The asipu used magic to treat sick people. Early Mesopotamians believed sickness was caused by committing a sin. Asipus tried to expel demons by using charms and spells. If they could not cure the illness, the asu tried his herbal remedies.

EVIDENCE OF SURGERY

Later, Mesopotamians realized that illness could be caused by things such as rotten food or too much alcohol. One 5,000-year-old skeleton shows the person had surgery to remove part of his skull, perhaps to relieve the symptoms of a headache.

TECHNICAL SPECS

- Mesopotamian religion banned the dissection of corpses.
- Doctors believed that emotions were located in the liver and intelligence in the heart.
- The first set of laws, the Code of Hammurabi (1700 B.C.E.), punished surgical mistakes by mutilation or death.
- The oldest medical text was written in 2100 B.C.E.
- Some remedies were related to the color of the disease: jaundice was treated with yellow medicine.
- One medical record lists 230 remedies. It describes a mixture of herbs and perhaps beetroot, cilantro, and parsley that was drunk or applied externally.
- After the Mesopotamians, medical knowledge stood still for 2,000 years, until the ancient Greeks.

TIMELINE

ALL DATES B.C.E.

c.5000 Farmers move from northern Mesopotamia to the flat plains of the south.

c.4000 Southern settlements begin to grow into towns, such as Ur.

c.3500 The first Mesopotamian towns grow into cities, with dense housing, royal palaces, and large temples.

c.3200 The wheel is invented in Mesopotamia.

c.3100 Cuneiform writing appears at Uruk.

c.3000 Metalworkers mix copper and tin to make bronze, which is used for tools and weapons.

c.2750 Under the First Dynasty of Ur, the city of Ur begins a period of dominance that will last over 250 years.

c.2500 Two Mesopotamian city-states, Lagash and Umma, fight the first recorded war.

c.2330 Sumer is conquered by King Sargon, the ruler of Akkad.

c.2112 King Ur-Nammu founds the Third Dynasty of Sumer and throws off the rule of the foreign Gutians, who had conquered Sumer and Akkad.

c.2095 The throne of Ur passes to King Shulgi, who builds the city's Great Ziggurat.

c.2000 Ur is overthrown by the Elamites, from the east.

c.2000 Weapons are made from bronze.

c.1900 A desert people known as the Amorites conquer a large part of Mesopotamia; they make Babylon their capital.

c.1792 King Hammurabi comes to the throne in Babylon. He takes over Sumer and Akkad, as well as part of Assyria.

c.1783 Ur is attacked and destroyed by the Babylonians.

c.1600 Much of Mesopotamia is conquered by foreign peoples, the Hittites, and the Kassites.

c.1570 The Kassites found a dynasty that will rule Babylon for nearly 500 years.

c.1500 Two-wheeled war chariots are invented.

c.1500 The first-known glass is made in Mesopotamia.

c.1000 The Mesopotamians begin making iron weapons.

c.1000 The Mesopotamians develop their own alphabet, based on that of the Phoenicians.

c.950 The Assyrians of northern Mesopotamia begin a campaign of conquest that will eventually create a large empire in Mesopotamia and what is now Turkey.

c.612 Babylon rises to power again after the fall of the Assyrian empire. The new power is referred to as Neo-Babylonian, or "new Babylonian."

605 Nebuchadnezzar II comes to the throne in Babylon. He builds the city's famous Hanging Gardens. He also expands the Neo-Babylonian empire, conquering Syria, Palestine, and Jerusalem.

539 The Persian ruler Cyrus the Great conquers the Babylonian empire.

331 The Macedonian Alexander the Great overthrows the Persian empire and takes over Mesopotamia.

GLOSSARY

bitumen A substance related to petroleum that was used as a fuel and as a kind of waterproof tar.

canal An artificial waterway.

cast To pour molten metal into a mold and allow it to harden.

chariot A fast, two-wheeled, horse-drawn vehicle, used in warfare.

city-state A political unit ruled by a powerful city.

cuneiform "Wedge-shaped;" used to describe writing in which characters were pressed with a wedge-shaped nib into soft clay.

cylinder seal A carved stone tube that was rolled over soft clay to leave a design that identified the owner.

eclipse When one heavenly body prevents the light from another from reaching Earth.

empire A large territory ruled by an emperor or empress.

glaze A thin covering added to clay to make it shiny.

hemp A plant whose fibers are used to make material.

horoscope An attempt to tell the future based on the movement of the planets and stars.

irrigation Artificially watering fields to enable crops to grow.

kiln A very hot oven used to harden pottery or bake bricks.

linchpin A pin at the end of an axle to stop a wheel from falling off as it turns.

siege engine A large machine used to attack the walls of a besieged city.

theorem A mathematical idea that has been demonstrated to be true

vault An arched structure that forms a ceiling or roof.

ziggurat A tall building or temple that rose in a series of stories, each smaller than the one below.

zodiac A circular band that contains 12 astrological signs.

FURTHER INFORMATION

BOOKS

Bancroft-Hunt, Norman. *Living in Ancient Mesopotamia* (Living in the Ancient World). Chelsea House Publications, 2008.

Faiella, Graham. *Technology of Ancient Mesopotamia* (Technology of the Ancient World). Rosen Central, 2005.

Scholl, Elisabeth J. *Ancient Mesopotamia* (How'd They Do That?). Mitchell Lane Publishers, 2009.

Steele, Philip. *Mesopotamia* (DY Eyewitness Books). DK Children, 2007.

Woods, Michael. *Ancient Agricultural Technology: From Sickles to Plows* (Technology in Ancient Cultures). Twenty-First Century Books, 2011.

WEBSITES

ancienthistory.about.com/od/southasia/a/Sumer.htm/
About.com introduction to the civilization of Sumer.

sunearthday.nasa.gov/2006/locations/babylon.php
Page on Babylonian astronomy from the NASA magazine Sun-Earth Day.

www.mesopotamia.co.uk/staff/resources/background/bg07/home.html
British Museum teachers' page about Mesopotamian technology.

www.anciv.info/mesopotamia/
Ancient Civilizations guide to Mesopotamia, including technology.

INDEX